lemonade lists

TURN YOUR LEMONS
INTO LEMONADE

a gratitude journal

AUTHOR CAROL FRAZIER

ILLUSTRATIONS BY CINDY BRIGGS

Copyright © 2025 by Carol Frazier

No part of this book may be reproduced in any form or by any electronic or mechanical means, or the facilitation thereof, including information storage and retrieval systems, without permission in writing from the publisher, except in the case of brief quotations published in articles and reviews. Any educational institution wishing to photocopy part or all of the work for classroom use, or individual researchers who would like to obtain permission to reprint the work for educational purposes, should contact the publisher.

ISBN: 978-1-966369-12-7
Library of Congress Control Number: 2025905387

Designed by Sami Langston
Project managed by Erin Harpst

Printed in the United States of America

Published by
Belle Isle Books (an imprint of Brandylane Publishers, Inc.)
5 S. 1st Street
Richmond, Virginia 23219

BELLE ISLE BOOKS
www.belleislebooks.com

belleislebooks.com | brandylanepublishers.com

life is a journey of turning
our lemons into lemonade

it begins with a choice to
slice into that first lemon
and put on the squeeze

− Carol Frazier

gratitude

gratefulness

thankfulness

looking for the good,
finding the silver lining

rising above the
darkness of depression
with gratitude

Let's Make Some Lemonade!

Someone once famously said life is like a box of chocolates—but in reality, I've found life is more like a bowl of fruit. As you look into your bowl of life, you may recall the taste of the sweet cherry memories that filled your childhood. You might remember the fun banana-split days of summer and apple-pie family memories.

Maybe your bowl has been filled with more lemons than sweet fruit. Do you pucker up when you think about your past hurdles or current difficulties? Maybe life has soured you and made you scared to dream. Maybe you have forgotten the magic of childhood.

I'm sure you've heard another famous saying: "When life gives you lemons, make lemonade!" And that is just what children do: they squeeze those lemons, mix in the sugar, and go sell lemonade on the corner. "Come to me as little children," exclaimed Jesus, reminding us to approach life with a playful and hopeful heart.

Gratitude is the sugar in your lemonade! When we focus on gratitude, we add sweetness to our day, while bitterness and sour thoughts are chased away.

The Lemonade Lists are designed to remind you of your joy, your passion, your dreams, and past miracles; and to anchor you in your appreciation of today. Lemonade Lists help you identify small daily miracles to shift your perception from sour, burnt out, hurt, and overwhelmed to a place of gratitude. They are simple lists, because gratitude is simple; but they are also powerful, for it is the daily practice of gratitude and positive feelings that help us keep our personal lemonade stands open. As you play with the lists, you will once again see the silver lining in your life, and sadness will wash away.

I'm not just saying that—my own experience has shown me how effective these daily practices can be. As a recovered feeling-sorry-for-myself, depressed, victimized, anxiety-ridden, and basically not-fun-to-be-around sour lemon myself, I discovered that creating gratitude lists, learning to love myself, and recognizing the little ways I could give back inspired a miraculous shift in my own perspective on life. In my journey to recover from serious PTSD caused by abuse, I found that daily gratitude was my single most powerful tool in finding joy and peace inside my seriously troubled heart. I am eternally grateful to the lemon presses that entered my life, squeezed the gratefulness from me, and taught me how to add sugar once again.

Lemonade Lists is full of photos, paintings, and recipes from my best "squeezers." These are the people who loved me back to a state of gratitude and health. I am forever grateful for their talents, and for the tough love that helped open this lemonade stand for you.

Ultimately, we all get to create our own lives, and choose the thoughts, dreams and hopes that make them sweet. I trust that in creating your own Lemonade Lists, you too will reclaim your spirit of joy and be able to pass along your gratitude at your lemonade stand of happiness.

hugs,
Carol

How This Book Works

This book is a creative space where you can create your own lists—some based on unique prompts, others based on consistent reminders to practice three aspects of a healthy life: gratitude, self-love, and generosity. Along with inspirational quotes and pictures, these lists will help you shift your perspective to one of growth, happiness, and appreciation—of yourself, your life, and the lives of those around you.

three gratitudes

This book offers space for you to write down three gratitudes every day. This is the most important intention you should hold for yourself. There is power in actually writing it down with your hand, creating a tactile and visual reminder for your brain and spirit that you are choosing gratitude each and every day. The gratitudes can be as simple as one word, or as elaborate as a paragraph describing your gratitude.

Here are some examples:

health
job
family
home

I am grateful for my health, and that I am still active and able to play with my children.

I am grateful for my gifts and talents, and that I can use them to inspire others.

I am grateful for my family, and for the support that we give each other.

I am grateful for my small, cozy home, because there is less space to clean than in a big home!

"Think it and ink it" is a powerful saying that aligns your thoughts and intentions for a positive and happy life. Writing down three gratitudes can be just a small step toward your own journal of joy and happy daily musings. You will be amazed at how such a tiny step of gratefulness will open the door to healing.

Have you ever filled journals of thoughts like "Woe is me; poor me; I can't stand so-and-so"... and so on? Pay attention to when you think these negative thoughts compared to your gratitude thoughts. You will start to feel the difference in your body.

The body's physical response to thoughts is amazing! And intentions are fueled by feelings. So, feed yourself a course in daily gratitudes.

> gratitude is the sugar in my lemonade
> – Carol Frazier

three Self-loves
gratitudes toward myself

Here lies a deep challenge, if you dare take it: Can you come up with three things you love about yourself every single day—three gratitudes toward yourself?

Imagine asking a child, "What do you like best about being you?" First, they might look at you funny, not quite understanding the question—because their world revolves around them, and of course they like themselves! They can easily rattle off what they are good at and what they love. They haven't yet been broken down or hurt by harsh words or lost dreams. Do you think the children contemplated whether they were good enough before they made their lemonade and set up a stand on the corner? Did they do a market analysis and get a makeover before they sold smiles to the neighbors?

During hard times, most of us have a tough time loving ourselves. Writing down what you love about yourself will stretch you toward a new horizon. Approaching your life with gratitude toward yourself will enlighten you, and lighten the load of self-torturing negative thoughts. Just give it a try—you might actually find yourself learning to love who you were created to be.

Your gratitudes toward yourself might look like these:

I like my hair today. I am enjoying my natural curls.

I love the soup I made last night. I am a good cook.

I love that I am challenging myself to become more flexible.

Gratitude about how you took care of yourself on a prior occasion works too:

I went to a deep stretch yoga class and got in touch with my body.

I got all dressed up today and I felt good about myself.

I watched a video on eating healthy food.

loving yourself first is the best way to love others
— Carol Frazier

three generosities
how I gave away my lemonade

Generosities are where we drop all pretenses that the world revolves around us, and instead foster our awareness of others. They remind us of what we have given back to others—of times we were generous with our attention and kind to those around us. You give back every day, whether you know it or not—with gestures as simple as a smile, a hug, or a word of encouragement. Writing down how you were a blessing to someone else brings the sentiment "Love yourself so you can love your neighbor" full circle.

Why do you have to record these moments? To bring a habit of gratefulness and awareness to your daily push through life. By writing them down, you recognize the times that you add sugar to someone's lemons.

Here are some examples:

I sent hugs and love texts to my daughter yesterday.

I made soup for a friend who was ill.

I walked my dog and let him run in the park.

Train your mind, and your heart will follow. By writing down these three simple lists every day, you will pour so much sugar on your lemons that you will have the sweetest and most refreshing lemonade of anyone you know, and your lemonade stand will be the happiest stand on the corner.

life is sweeter when I sprinkle it with generosity and love
– Carol Frazier

Lemonade Lists

These lists are all about finding your happiness. They are for you to find your joy and fill up on happy thoughts. They were created for you to play with—however and whenever it feels right. You may want to go from page to page, following a daily routine, or you may get all juiced up from moving around the book to your heart's content.

Blank pages have been included throughout the book to allow you to create your own lists and journal. Be creative, draw pictures, color, and play! There are no rules. I only suggest that you find a few minutes every day to write down your three gratitudes, self-loves, and generosities.

Keep this journal close, in a place where you can find it every day—by your bed, in your purse, or in your backpack. Scribble, paint, and create to turn your lemons into lemonade and establish a healthy journal and life full of sugary happy thoughts!

Go explore!

Extras

Everyone loves lemon recipes! So I "squeezed" some lemony recipes by my executive chef husband, Timothy Ramirez, into this book. Illustrations by internationally known artist Cindy Briggs are also included, to inspire and lift your spirits. I even threw in a few of my own creations. See if you can find them!

Finally, at the back of this book, you will see more empty journal pages for you to fill in whatever way you choose. Draw, write, dream, hope, and continue your expressive journey on these pages.

gratitudes

1. _____

2. _____

3. _____

self-loves

1. _____

2. _____

3. _____

generosities

1. _____

2. _____

3. _____

nothing is
so strong as
gentleness,

nothing so gentle
as real strength

— Saint Francis
de Sales

only the gentle
are ever really
strong

— James Dean

list five ways to be more gentle with yourself today

1. _____

   _____

2. _____

   _____

3. _____

   _____

4. _____

   _____

5. _____

   _____

gratitudes

1. _____
2. _____
3. _____

self-loves

1. _____
2. _____
3. _____

generosities

1. _____
2. _____
3. _____

As a child, what did you want to be when you grew up?

_____

_____

_____

_____

_____

_____

_____

_____

gratitudes

1. _____
2. _____
3. _____

self-loves

1. _____
2. _____
3. _____

generosities

1. _____
2. _____
3. _____

may the window
of your soul

open to the dreams
of your heart

– Carol Frazier

list three ways
you plan to enjoy your day today

1. _____

   _____

2. _____

   _____

3. _____

   _____

gratitudes

1. _____
2. _____
3. _____

self-loves

1. _____
2. _____
3. _____

generosities

1. _____
2. _____
3. _____

ingredients

- 2 cups butter, softened
- ⅔ cup powdered sugar
- 1 tsp. grated lemon zest
- ½ tsp. vanilla
- 1 ¾ cups flour
- Gluten-Free Substitute:
    - 1 cup almond flour +
    - ¾ cup coconut flour
- 1 ½ cups cornstarch

creamy lemon glaze

- 4 tbsp butter, melted
- 1 tsp. grated lemon zest
- ⅓ cup lemon juice
- 2 ½ cups powdered sugar

Combine butter, zest, juice, and powdered sugar. Stir.

instructions

Preheat the oven to 350°F.

In a small bowl, beat butter until creamy.

Add powdered sugar and mix until light and fluffy. Add lemon zest and vanilla. Beat well.

Add flour and cornstarch, and mix until combined.

Roll dough into one-inch balls and bake for 15 minutes on a greased cookie sheet, until the bottom edges of the cookies are light brown.

Cool on wax paper and frost with lemon glaze.

gratitudes

1. _____
2. _____
3. _____

self-loves

1. _____
2. _____
3. _____

generosities

1. _____
2. _____
3. _____

list three "I cannot's"

1. _____

   _____

2. _____

   _____

3. _____

   _____

restate your "I cannot's" as three "I can's"

_____

_____

_____

_____

_____

Examples: *I can't dance* can be turned into: I would like to learn at least one dance for an upcoming event.

I can't leave can be turned into: I can ask for help leaving this situation.

gratitudes

1. _____
2. _____
3. _____

self-loves

1. _____
2. _____
3. _____

generosities

1. _____
2. _____
3. _____

Fresh Squeezed Lemonade

ingredients

13 lemons, 1 for garnish

1 cup boiling water

2 cups sugar

water

ice cubes

lemon drop candies

instructions

Bring 1 cup of water to a boil. Place sugar into a large bowl. Pour boiling water over 2 cups sugar and stir until dissolved. Squeeze the juice of 12 lemons into a gallon-sized pitcher filled with cold water and ice cubes. Cut the last lemon into slices and add it to the pitcher.

Place 30 lemon drop candies in a freezer bag. Crush with a hammer until the consistency resembles rock salt. Pour the crushed candies onto a plate. Invert glasses and dip the rims in ¼ inch water or lemon juice. Then dip the rims into the crushed candies.

_____

_____

_____

gratitudes

1. _____
2. _____
3. _____

self-loves

1. _____
2. _____
3. _____

generosities

1. _____
2. _____
3. _____

My Favorites

Finish these sentences.

My favorite color is . . .

_____

My favorite smell is . . .

_____

My favorite sound is . . .

_____

My favorite flavor is . . .

_____

My favorite drink is . . .

_____

My favorite food is . . .

_____

My favorite song is …

_____

My favorite movie is …

_____

My favorite book is …

_____

My favorite character is …

_____

My favorite person is …

_____

My favorite animal is …

_____

My favorite activity is …

_____

it's never too
late for a

new beginning
in your life

— Joyce Meyers

gratitudes

1. _____
2. _____
3. _____

self-loves

1. _____
2. _____
3. _____

generosities

1. _____
2. _____
3. _____

the journey
to your dreams
begins with
one small step

- Carol Frazier

The Journey

Where I am now . . .

_____
_____
_____
_____
_____

Where I want to be . . .

_____
_____
_____
_____
_____

How I want to get there . . .

_____

_____

_____

What I want to experience . . .

_____

_____

_____

How I want to feel . . .

_____

_____

_____

What first small step I can take . . .

_____

_____

_____

gratitudes

1. _____

2. _____

3. _____

self-loves

1. _____

2. _____

3. _____

generosities

1. _____

2. _____

3. _____

write down one project that gets priority today

_____

what is one small step you can take toward your goal?

_____

_____

gratitudes

1. _____
2. _____
3. _____

self-loves

1. _____
2. _____
3. _____

generosities

1. _____
2. _____
3. _____

Best Friends

Who are your best friends whom you can trust during both the sweet times and the sour times in life?

1. _____

2. _____

3. _____

4. _____

> true friends aren't the ones who make your problems disappear; they are the ones who won't disappear when you're facing problems
>
> — Unknown

gratitudes

1. _____
2. _____
3. _____

self-loves

1. _____
2. _____
3. _____

generosities

1. _____
2. _____
3. _____

Lift your spirits

List seven ways you can raise your energy and happiness levels if you are feeling emotionally down or in a slump.

1. _____

2. _____

3. _____

4. _____

5. _____

6. _____

7. _____

gratitudes

1. _____
2. _____
3. _____

self-loves

1. _____
2. _____
3. _____

generosities

1. _____
2. _____
3. _____

list three ways

you can be the light for others

1. _____

   _____

2. _____

   _____

3. _____

   _____

it is during
our darkest
moments

that we must
focus on
the light

— Aristotle Onassis

gratitudes

1. _____
2. _____
3. _____

self-loves

1. _____
2. _____
3. _____

generosities

1. _____
2. _____
3. _____

list three ways that you
are present in the "here and now"

1. _____

   _____

2. _____

   _____

3. _____

   _____

gratitudes

1. _____
2. _____
3. _____

self-loves

1. _____
2. _____
3. _____

generosities

1. _____
2. _____
3. _____

List your Dream Vacations

Tropical islands, exotic cities, familiar places, or a simple staycation at home with someone you love.

List your dream vacations here:

1. _____

2. _____

3. _____

4. _____

5. _____

6. _____

7. _____

whoever is happy

will make others happy too!

– Anne Frank

gratitudes

1. _____
2. _____
3. _____

self-loves

1. _____
2. _____
3. _____

generosities

1. _____
2. _____
3. _____

list seven happy memories

1. _____

   _____

2. _____

   _____

3. _____

   _____

4. _____

_____

5. _____

_____

6. _____

_____

7. _____

_____

gratitudes

1. _____
2. _____
3. _____

self-loves

1. _____
2. _____
3. _____

generosities

1. _____
2. _____
3. _____

your sacred space is
where you can find
yourself
over and over again

— Joseph Campbell

to whom do you give your energy?

We all give and take energy to those around us every day. For example, a young mother gives energy and time to her small children—but when those children curl up in her lap at the end of the day and smile at her, she receives energy back.

To whom are you giving energy? Who is taking your energy without giving energy back? Who is squeezing the lemon juice right out of you?

Reflect here, and list a few people or even things that are leaving you dry—and a few people or things that are filling you up.

_____
_____
_____
_____
_____
_____
_____
_____
_____
_____
_____
_____
_____
_____
_____

gratitudes

1. _____
2. _____
3. _____

self-loves

1. _____
2. _____
3. _____

generosities

1. _____
2. _____
3. _____

The Gratitude Rock

Go outside and find a rock that is small enough to fit in your pocket. The rock should feel wonderful in the palm of your hand as you carry it, and feel good between your fingers as you hold it.

In the morning, put the rock in your pocket and carry it with you throughout the day. Every time you find yourself touching the stone, think of something you are grateful for.

In the evening, put the rock beside your bed. Repeat this exercise as long as it feels right.

gratitudes

1. _____
2. _____
3. _____

self-loves

1. _____
2. _____
3. _____

generosities

1. _____
2. _____
3. _____

keep your head
above the
clouds;

the view is
better up here

— Carol Frazier

list three larger-than-life dreams

1. _____

   _____

2. _____

   _____

3. _____

   _____

Dreams in the Clouds

How would your life change

if even one of these dreams came true?

_____

_____

_____

_____

_____

_____

_____

_____

_____

_____

_____

_____

_____

_____

_____

_____

How would you feel if this dream came true?

What would it look like?

gratitudes

1. _____
2. _____
3. _____

self-loves

1. _____
2. _____
3. _____

generosities

1. _____
2. _____
3. _____

Look into the mirror today

Hug yourself . . .

Smile at yourself . . .

Keep smiling until you feel yourself smile inside . . .

Feel gratitude toward your body . . .

Write down what you are most grateful for in your mind, body, and spirit.

mind
_____
_____
_____

body
_____
_____
_____

spirit
_____
_____
_____

gratitudes

1. _____

2. _____

3. _____

self-loves

1. _____

2. _____

3. _____

generosities

1. _____

2. _____

3. _____

Doodle your gratitudes today!

do unto others
as you would have them
do unto you

— the golden Rule

list three ways you want others to treat you

1. _____

   _____

2. _____

   _____

3. _____

   _____

gratitudes

1. _____
2. _____
3. _____

self-loves

1. _____
2. _____
3. _____

generosities

1. _____
2. _____
3. _____

Lemon Poppy Seed Cake

ingredients

- 4 cups cake flour
- 2 tsp. baking powder
- 1 ½ tsp. baking soda
- 1 tsp. salt
- 1 cup butter
- 1 ½ cups sugar
- 2 tsp. vanilla
- 1 ½ tsp. almond extract
- 4 large eggs
- 2 cups buttermilk
- 3 tbsp. poppy seeds

instructions

Preheat the oven to 350°F. Combine flour, baking powder, baking soda, and salt in a large bowl and set aside.

In a separate bowl, cream together butter and sugar. Add eggs, vanilla, and almond extract, and cream until fluffy. Add buttermilk and mix. Slowly add dry ingredients while mixing. Add poppy seeds last, folding them in.

Pour the batter into two greased 9-inch round cake pans and bake for 30 minutes or until a toothpick comes out clean. While the cake is baking, make lemon glaze and lemon cream cheese filling.

notes

_____

_____

_____

_____

lemon glaze

- ¼ cup butter
- 2 lemons, juiced and zested
- 1 cup sugar

Combine butter, juice, zest, and sugar in a small saucepan. Cook on low until sugar is dissolved.

Lemon Cream Cheese Filling

- 8 oz. soft cream cheese
- ½ cup butter, softened
- 3 tbsp. fresh lemon juice
- 2-2 ½ cups powdered sugar

Add all ingredients to a food processor or an electric mixer and blend until well incorporated.

instructions, cont.

Let cakes cool in a pan for 15 minutes. Invert and cool on a rack for another 15 minutes. Place first cake onto a cake platter. Poke holes in the cake with a fork and pour half the glaze on top, letting it soak into the cake.

Spread a layer of cream cheese frosting onto the cake, then place the second cake on top. Poke holes in this second layer and pour on the remaining lemon glaze.

Frost the top of the cake with lemon cream cheese frosting, letting some drip down the sides. Serve with fresh raspberries.

Enjoy!

gratitudes

1. _____
2. _____
3. _____

self-loves

1. _____
2. _____
3. _____

generosities

1. _____
2. _____
3. _____

list three of your favorite ways to exercise

1. _____

   _____

2. _____

   _____

3. _____

   _____

list three new physical activities you can try this month

1. _____
   _____

2. _____
   _____

3. _____
   _____

gratitudes

1. _____
2. _____
3. _____

self-loves

1. _____
2. _____
3. _____

generosities

1. _____
2. _____
3. _____

take care of
your body . . .

it is the only
place you
have to live

— Jim Rohn

the Healthy grocery list

Food is the fuel for our bodies, so what we eat is extremely important! We all can make wiser choices when it comes to fueling our bodies. In the space below, list three foods or beverages you will avoid purchasing during your next grocery run.

1. _____

2. _____

3. _____

1. _____

2. _____

3. _____

list seven healthy food choices

What are seven healthy foods and drinks you will buy to have on hand for healthy eating? Remember, if it's there and easy to grab, you can make a healthy choice.

1. _____

2. _____

3. _____

4. _____

5. _____

6. _____

7. _____

gratitudes

1. _____
2. _____
3. _____

self-loves

1. _____
2. _____
3. _____

generosities

1. _____
2. _____
3. _____

the Ultimate Bucket List

List seven things you want to do in your lifetime.

Don't let time, money, or anything else hold you back.

The sky's the limit!

1. _____

2. _____

3. _____

4. _____

5. _____

6. _____

7. _____

all our dreams can come true, if we have the courage to pursue them

— Walt Disney

gratitudes

1. _____

2. _____

3. _____

self-loves

1. _____

2. _____

3. _____

generosities

1. _____

2. _____

3. _____

the *"I have too much to do"* list

We all get overwhelmed sometimes—even with our to-do lists! Use this list to help yourself get organized.

1. _____

2. _____

3. _____

4. _____

5. _____

6. _____

7. _____

8. _____

9. _____

10. _____

11. _____

12. _____

13. _____

14. _____

Downsizing

What can I finish today?

1. _____

2. _____

3. _____

simplify, simplify, simplify

— Henry David Thoreau

one 'simplify' would have sufficed

- Ralph Waldo Emerson

gratitudes

1. _____
2. _____
3. _____

self-loves

1. _____
2. _____
3. _____

generosities

1. _____
2. _____
3. _____

Lemon Meringue Pie

ingredients

- dough for a single-crust pie, rolled into a 12-inch circle ⅛ of an inch thick
- 8 large eggs
- 2 cups + 2 tbsp. sugar
- ¼ cup cornstarch
- 1 cup fresh lemon juice
- ¼ tsp. fine sea salt
- 4 tbsp. unsalted butter, cut into tablespoons
- zest of 3 lemons, finely grated

instructions

Place the dough round into a 9-inch pie dish, fitting it to the bottom and sides. Trim the dough, leaving a ¾-inch overhang. Flute the overhanging dough over the edge of the pie dish. Using a fork, pierce the dough all over, and freeze for 30 minutes.

While the dough is cooling, position a rack in the lower third of an oven and preheat to 375°F. Place the dough-lined dish on a baking sheet and fill the foil with pie weights. Bake until the dough looks dry and is barely golden, 12 to 15 minutes. Remove the foil and weights.

Continue baking until the crust is golden brown, 12 to 15 minutes more. Transfer to a rack and cool while you make the filling. Raise the oven temperature to 400°F.

In a bowl, beat 3 of the eggs until blended. Separate the remaining 5 eggs, adding the yolks to the beaten whole eggs and putting the whites in a separate large bowl. Cover the whites and set aside at room temperature. Beat the yolks into the beaten eggs. In another bowl, whisk together 1½ cups of the sugar and the cornstarch, then whisk in the beaten eggs, lemon juice, and salt.

Transfer to a heavy, nonreactive saucepan, place over medium heat, and heat until the mixture comes to a full boil, whisking almost constantly. This can also be done in a double-broiler to avoid burning (place saucepan into a larger saucepan with ½ inch of water).

instructions, cont.

Reduce heat to low and let bubble for 30 seconds. Be careful not to undercook or overcook the filling, or it will separate as it cools. Remove from heat and whisk in the butter. Strain through a coarse-mesh sieve into a bowl to remove any bits of cooked egg white. Stir in the lemon zest, then pour into the baked crust. (The crust can be warm or cool.)

Using a handheld mixer on high speed, beat the reserve egg whites until soft peaks form. One tablespoon at a time, beat in the remaining ½ cup plus 2 tbsp. sugar, beating until the egg whites form shiny, stiff peaks.

Using a rubber spatula, spread the meringue evenly over the hot filling, making sure the meringue touches the crust on all sides to prevent it from shrinking. Swirl the meringue with the spatula to form peaks. Bake at 400°F until the meringue is browned, about 5 minutes. Transfer to a rack and cool completely before serving, at least 3 hours.

Serves 8.

gratitudes

1. _____
2. _____
3. _____

self-loves

1. _____
2. _____
3. _____

generosities

1. _____
2. _____
3. _____

Giving Back

To whom can you give unselfishly today?

1. _____

2. _____

3. _____

4. _____

5. _____

only a life lived for others
is a life worthwhile

— Albert Einstein

gratitudes

1. _____

2. _____

3. _____

self-loves

1. _____

2. _____

3. _____

generosities

1. _____

2. _____

3. _____

The Silver Lining

During difficult times, it's hard to see the silver lining. List three difficult experiences you are going through today, and then find the silver lining in each of them.

1. _____

silver lining _____

2. _____

silver lining _____

3. _____

silver lining _____

gratitudes

1. _____
2. _____
3. _____

self-loves

1. _____
2. _____
3. _____

generosities

1. _____
2. _____
3. _____

the Perfect Day

If you could describe your perfect day, what would it be?

gratitudes

1. _____
2. _____
3. _____

self-loves

1. _____
2. _____
3. _____

generosities

1. _____
2. _____
3. _____

when life gets too hot, let gratitude be your umbrella

— Carol Frazier

Final thoughts

We hope you have had a wonderful experience creating gratitude with the Lemonade Lists, and that gratitude and happy thoughts can come with ease during good and bad times. We hope you can always turn your lemons into lemonade, and give it away freely to others in need of a helping hand or encouragement. Remember: you are the creator of your thoughts, and positivity and dreams come true through the door of gratitude.

If these Lemonade Lists have helped you in any way, who are three people with whom you would share the Lemonade Lists?

1. _____

2. _____

3. _____

Thank you for taking this journey with us!

Learn more at http://carolfrazier.com and http://cindybriggs.com.

Create a Great Day,

Carol Frazier & Cindy Briggs

About the Author

Carol Frazier is an impassioned artist dedicated to inspiring others as an accomplished recording artist, actress, screenwriter, author, speaker, and creative coach. She is the founder of Carol Frazier Studio, hosts the online summit Inspired Creativity, and provides artistic development for creatives.

Carol's own original music can be found on all streaming platforms, and spans four original albums: *Life's a Ride*, *Simple Baby Boy*, *Três*, and *Then Came You*; as well as three compilation albums. Her original compositions can also be found in film and TV.

After overcoming obstacles on her own personal journey, recovering, and healing with gratitude, Carol created the Lemonade Lists to encourage others to do the same—"making lemonade out of lemons." She also created several online courses and group programs to help people find their voice and follow their dreams: *Compose Yourself*; *Overcome Stage Fright and Heal Performance Anxiety*; and *The Sing Zone Method*, for which she has also written a book of the same name.

Carol is based in Carmel-by-the-Sea, CA; and Aspen, CO. You can visit her at carolfrazier.com.

Email: carolfrazierstudio@gmail.com
Instagram: @carolfrazierartist & @carolfrazierstudio
Facebook: www.facebook.com/carolfraziermusic
YouTube: www.youtube.com/@CarolFrazier
IMDB: https://www.imdb.com/name/nm12297539

about the artist

Cindy Briggs, NWS, NWWS, comes from a family of artists who are inspired to create and share their love of painting. Sharing her journey through watercolors, she blends light, emotion, and luminous color to leave a lasting impression.

As an international watercolor workshop instructor for twenty-five years, Cindy continues to lead *plein air* workshops throughout Europe and the United States. She also teaches online and studio workshops for Smithsonian Art Studios; Terracotta.art; and other leading arts organizations; as well as at the University of Utah, near her home. Encouraging artists at all levels, her numerous online programs offer accessible opportunities for creative growth.

Cindy is a Signature Member of the National (NWS) and Northwest Watercolor Societies (NWWS), as well as a Daniel Smith Watercolor Ambassador. Her work is featured in *Splash 24*, *Plein Air* magazine, *Outdoor Painter*, and *American Watercolor*.

"Collaborating on this project with my cousin, Carol, has been truly meaningful—it's always exciting to share our creative connection."

—Cindy Briggs

Email: CindyBriggsArt@gmail.com

Instagram: @cindybriggs

Facebook: www.facebook.com/CindyBriggsArt

YouTube: www.youtube.com/@CindyBriggs

Website: www.CindyBriggs.com

About the Chef

Culinary artist and award-winning chef Timothy Ramirez brings his passion for fresh ingredients to the innovative menus he has created over the years. After his four-year apprenticeship with master chefs from Europe, Tim was honored for his culinary prowess by none other than Jacques Pepin at the Scottsdale Culinary Festival. Tim took his creative skills to various fine dining locations both domestic and abroad. He has worked alongside some of the most skilled and renowned chefs from Europe.

Tim celebrates the beauty of ingredients in all his recipes, and enjoys staying current with the latest culinary trends. He speaks several languages, including English, Spanish, and Italian. In his spare time, Tim enjoys the outdoors with his wife Carol Frazier and their Aussiedoodle dog, Jack. Once an aspiring actor, writer, and producer, Tim has returned to his first love of writing screenplays.

Contact Timothy at timrinternational@gmail.com.

Workshops & Retreats

Carol Frazier, Cindy Briggs, and Timothy Ramirez find joy in inspiring others in creativity, art, music, creative writing, journaling, and travel. As a result, they delight in hosting creative and inspirational workshops and retreats around the world.

Creativity Retreats combine "bucket list" travel experiences, creative journaling, painting, music, cooking classes, and more. They are for those of us who find joy in exploring new places, meeting new people, and embracing life to the fullest.

To learn more about how you can attend a Creativity Retreat, visit Carol at www.carolfrazier.com or Cindy at www.cindybriggs.com.

"Creativity has been a part of my life since I was a child, but I never thought of myself as a writer or even an artist. Carol and Cindy opened my mind and eyes to another part of myself that I didn't know existed. I have implemented their techniques in my daily life, and look at being artistic through a whole new lens."

— Heather Daines, Tour Leader, French Escapade

Credits

Author	Carol Frazier
Artist	Cindy Briggs
Recipes	Timothy Ramirez
Design & Layout	Jordan Christopher
Photography & Additional Artwork (pgs. 28, 66, 70, 71, 80, 102, 104, 113, & 126)	Carol Frazier
Additional Artwork (pg. 111)	Ellie Weakley (Carol's mother & Cindy's aunt!)

thank you

to our circle of friends and family
who continue to encourage our creative journey.

www.ingramcontent.com/pod-product-compliance
Lightning Source LLC
Chambersburg PA
CBHW041246240426
43669CB00025B/2983